You Can Too!
Success
After Failure

Jody Jensen Shaffer, M.A.

Publishing Credits

Rachelle Cracchiolo, M.S.Ed., *Publisher*
Conni Medina, M.A.Ed., *Managing Editor*
Nika Fabienke, Ed.D., *Series Developer*
June Kikuchi, *Content Director*
Seth Rogers, *Editor*
Michelle Jovin, M.A., *Assistant Editor*
Lee Aucoin, *Senior Graphic Designer*

TIME For Kids and the TIME For Kids logo are registered trademarks of TIME Inc. Used under license.

Image Credits: Cover and p.1 Granger, NYC; p.4 Christinne Muschi/ Toronto Star via Getty Images; p.5 Hero Images Inc./Alamy Stock Photo; p.6 National Portrait Gallery; pp.6–7 Artokoloro Quint Lox Limited/Alamy Stock Photo; p.7 Pictorial Press Ltd/Alamy Stock Photo; p.8 Science Source; p.9 pp.34–39, "Recreations of a Philosopher," Harper's New Monthly Magazine Volume 0030 Issue 175 (December, 1864); p.10 Glasshouse Images/Alamy Stock Photo; p.11 Creative Commons Attribution 3.0 Unported by CTG Publishing www.ctgpublishing.com; p.12 (left) Edison, Thomas Alva. Phonograph. U.S. Patent US227679 filed December 19, 1941, and published February, 24, 1948, (right) Replica of the first phonograph, invented by Thomas Alva Edison (1847-1931) in 1877 (metal) (see also 260255), English School/Science Museum, London, UK/Bridgeman Images; p.14 Photo © 2014 J.B. Spector/Bridgeman Images; p.15 Smithsonian Institution Libraries; p.16 National Archives and Records Administration [595519]; p.17 Everett Collection Inc/Alamy Stock Photo; p.18 SPL/Science Source; p.19 Photo © PVDE/Bridgeman Images; p.20 Library of Congress [LC-DIG-highsm-13966]; p.21 Prisma Archivo/Alamy Stock Photo; pp.22, 22–23, 24, 25, 27 Bettmann/Getty Images; p.28 H. Armstrong Roberts/ Getty Images; p.31 Everett Collection Inc/Alamy Stock Photo; p.33 Shutterstock; p.34 (top) Photo courtesy of Allan Alcorn, (bottom) Creative Commons Public Domain Dedication 1.0 by Evan Amos; p.35 Yvonne Hemsey/Getty Images; p.37 David Friedman.

Library of Congress Cataloging-in-Publication Data

Names: Shaffer, Jody Jensen, author.
Title: You can too! : success after failure / Jody Jensen Shaffer, M.A.
Description: Huntington Beach, CA : Teacher Created Materials, [2018] | Audience: Grade 4 to 6. | Includes index.
Identifiers: LCCN 2017023527 (print) | LCCN 2017048147 (ebook) | ISBN 9781425854669 (eBook) | ISBN 9781425849900 (pbk.)
Subjects: LCSH: Inventions--Juvenile literature. | Success--Juvenile literature. | Perseverance (Ethics)--Juvenile literature.
Classification: LCC T14.7 (ebook) | LCC T14.7 .S53 2018 (print) | DDC 600--dc23
LC record available at https://lccn.loc.gov/2017023527

Teacher Created Materials

5301 Oceanus Drive
Huntington Beach, CA 92649-1030
http://www.tcmpub.com
ISBN 978-1-4258-4990-0
© 2018 Teacher Created Materials, Inc.

Table of Contents

If at First...

You've probably heard it before: "If at first you don't succeed, try, try again." But what if you don't succeed on the second try or even the hundredth? Should you still keep trying? Definitely, according to the people you'll read about in this book. They all had questions they wanted to answer or problems they wanted to solve. But they didn't succeed on their first attempts. They tried new methods and materials, or they waited for science or technology to catch up with them. Many faced **criticism** and **ridicule**, but these inventors kept trying until they achieved success.

The Snowmobile

In 1922, 15-year-old Joseph-Armand Bombardier (ARE-mone BOM-bar-deer) strapped the engine of a Model T Ford to two wooden sleds. His vehicle traveled well through the snow. But Bombardier's dad made him take it apart. He thought it wasn't safe. Bombardier didn't let that stop him. In 1935, he built the first successful (and safe) snowmobile.

À LA POURSUITE D'UN RÊVE
FOLLOWING A DREAM

Bombardier's first vehicle on display

1800s: Communication

Mark Twain once wrote, "The man with a new idea is a **crank** until the idea succeeds." The inventors in this chapter would probably agree.

Babbage's Difference Engine

Around 1820, Charles Babbage saw a set of math tables that sparked an idea. A Frenchman named Gaspard de Prony (gas-PAHR DEE proh-nee)made the tables years before. He had hired hundreds of people to form a single system of measurement. Babbage liked the way de Prony had split up the work. But Babbage thought a machine could do the job faster and better. So, he came up with the Difference Engine.

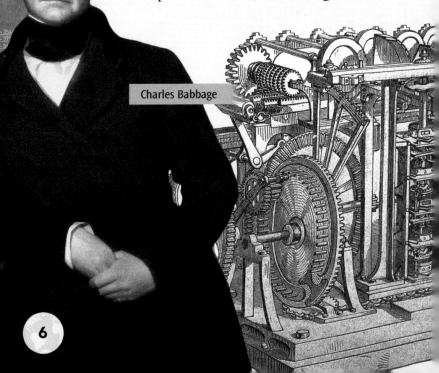

Charles Babbage

Making Her Mark

While building his machine, Babbage met a young woman named Ada Lovelace (shown below). She was amazed by Babbage's work. She had studied in London and was skilled in both math and science. Lovelace came up with a code for the engine that would allow it to handle letters and symbols as well as numbers, but it was never used. Some of her ideas are still used in computer programs today.

Babbage's Difference Engine could add and subtract. But, it could not multiply or divide. In 1832, Babbage built a **prototype**. He spent the next seven years working on his project. Then he ran out of money. He was **dejected**, but he did not give up. Instead, he started to work on an even better machine that he called the Analytical Engine.

The new machine could multiply and divide. But, Babbage could not afford to finish this machine, either. So, he began work on the Difference Engine 2. Years passed, but Babbage never finished any of his engines. Some people might see this as a failure. However, his inventions paved the way for others to develop today's computers.

Volta's Volts

Luigi Galvani (loo-EE-jee gal-VON-ee) saw that the legs of dead frogs twitched when they touched metal. He thought the animals contained electricity. Another man, Alessandro Volta (ah-lee-SAHN-droe VOL-tuh), did not agree. He proved it was the metals and wet cloths that were making electricity (now called *volts*). Volta had taken the first step in making a battery.

Alessandro Volta

STOP! THINK...

This is a drawing of Charles Babbage's Difference Engine, a machine designed to **compute** numbers.

> What other machines does this drawing remind you of?

> How might the history of computers be different if he had finished this machine?

> Why might people call Babbage the "Father of Modern Computers"?

CALCULATION COMPLETE

PORTION OF BABBAGE'S DIFFERENCE ENGINE.

Bell's "Harmonic Telegraph"

Alexander Graham Bell first called the telephone a "harmonic **telegraph**." That means a telegraph that speaks. In 1876, he used it to say a short message to his assistant in another room. "Mr. Watson, come here. I want to see you."

What did the world think of Bell's invention? Western Union said they thought the telephone had "too many **shortcomings**" to be useful. The chief engineer of the British Post Office said, "The Americans have need of the telephone, but we do not. We have plenty of messenger boys." Today, over six billion people have access to cell phones.

Messenger Boys

When someone sent a telegraph, the message was received in a telegraph office. From there, messenger boys took the telegraph to the person it was meant for. These boys were as young as 14 years old. Their jobs could be dangerous as they rode their bicycles or motorbikes through the cities to deliver their notes.

Not in My Office

Alexander Graham Bell invented the telephone, but he did not want to have one in his study. He was afraid it would be too much of a distraction. He wanted to stay focused on his scientific work. A phone, distracting? Nah!

Edison's Bright Idea

In the late 1800s, several people were working on an **alternative** to gaslight for their homes and offices. At that time, the only source of light in the dark came from candles, gas lamps, or oil lamps. Thomas Edison was one of the people trying to find a new option.

Edison wanted to make a light bulb that would last. But it was not easy! The tiny **filament** inside the bulb kept burning out. He had to find a solution. Edison tried many different materials. Platinum cost too much, and cotton thread could not stand the heat for long. Then, in 1879, he found the perfect fit. After years of trial and error, electric lights were born!

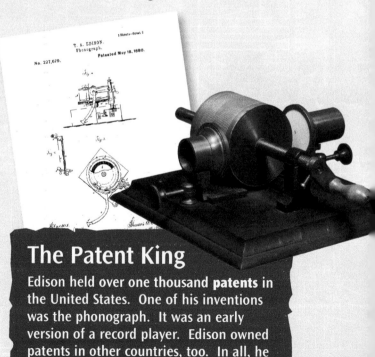

The Patent King

Edison held over one thousand **patents** in the United States. One of his inventions was the phonograph. It was an early version of a record player. Edison owned patents in other countries, too. In all, he owned over two thousand patents!

THINK LINK

> Why would someone want to be an inventor?

> How do people become inventors?

> What are some characteristics inventors need to be successful?

Thomas Edison

13

Marconi's Radio

For years, people used **Morse code** and telegraphs to communicate. Miles of telegraph wires crisscrossed lands. In 1894, Italian inventor Guglielmo Marconi (goo-lee-EL-moe mar-KOH-nee) found a way to send messages without wires. He used radio waves. He told the Minister of Posts and Telegraphs about his idea. But, the minister thought it could not be done. He tried to send Marconi to an **asylum**. Even Edison thought the "radio craze" would die out.

But Marconi would not give up. He learned more and more about how radio waves worked. Six years later, he got his patent. People could now send messages around the world without using a single wire!

Hello, Operator

If you wanted to make a phone call before 1889, an operator would place the call for you. That's when Almon Strowger (ALL-mawn STROE-jer) noticed he was losing business. He found out that the wife of one of his **rivals** was an operator. She was sending all the calls to her husband! So, Strowger invented switches to direct calls. Callers could dial directly, without an operator.

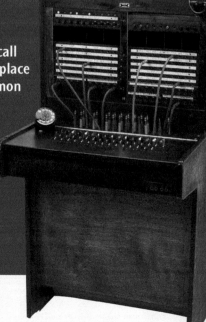

Missed Chances

In the beginning, Marconi (shown above) sold his invention to the military. But David Sarnoff, a manager at a radio company, thought everybody could use a radio. He asked his bosses to **invest**. But they would not budge. They said, "Who would pay for a message sent to nobody?"

Early 1900s: Convenience

Thanks to the inventors of the early 1900s, life became more convenient. Because of them, we can fly across the world, keep cool during summer, and pop a bag of delicious popcorn.

Carrier's Air Conditioner

It was hot and **humid** in New York in 1902. It was so hot that the ink on the cover of *Judge* magazine was sliding off the paper. Something had to be done, so the printer hired a man named Willis Carrier to cool down the printing shop. He worked day and night without success. A few weeks later, he came up with an idea. He could cool the room by passing air through cold coils. *Judge* was saved, and Carrier began an air conditioning company.

Stolen Success

In 1903, Elizabeth Magie (mah-ZHEE) patented a game called the *Landlord's Game*. The game was not a success, and Magie only made about $500. Think of her surprise when the same game was released years later under the name *Monopoly*. A man named Charles Darrow had stolen Magie's game and claimed it as his own. It wasn't until 1973 that the true inventor was uncovered and given credit.

Willis Carrier stands with his first air conditioner.

X-rays and Shoes

Wilhelm Roentgen (WILL-helm RENG-guhn) first discovered X-rays in 1895. He X-rayed his wife's hand and wedding ring. It shocked her so much that she told him, "I have seen my death." X-rays were first used in shoe stores to make sure shoes fit well. Stores continued to X-ray feet until the 1960s, when X-rays were banned because they leaked **radiation**. Later, they were improved and used in hospitals.

Wrights' Flight

When Orville and Wilbur Wright were children, their father bought them a toy helicopter. After that, the two brothers were **fascinated** by flight. As young men, they decided they wanted to invent a flying machine that could carry a person. They studied for years and finally built a **glider** in 1900, but it did not perform well.

Orville and Wilbur kept trying new ideas for the next year. In 1901, they created a second glider, but it did worse than the first. Still, they did not give up, and they built a third version the next year. It did well, but they knew they could still do better.

How Now, Cow?

In 1933, a farmer visited a scientist named Karl Paul Link (shown right). Any time the farmer's cows cut themselves, the farmer had a hard time getting them to heal. It took Link three years, but he discovered what was causing this to happen to the cows, which led to the discovery of blood thinners. The cows were saved. Link's medicine is still used to prevent heart attacks and **strokes**.

Orville and Wilbur Wright

Impossible Flight

In 1902, an **astronomer** named Simon Newcomb was reported to have said that flight by machines that are heavier than air could not be done. Within three years, the Wright brothers would prove him wrong!

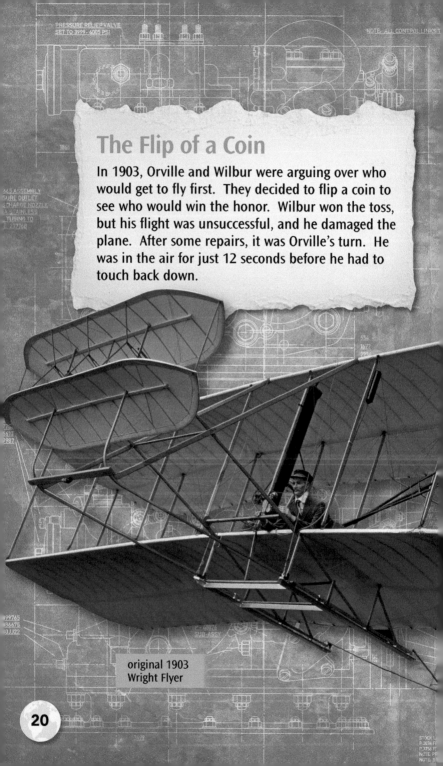

The Flip of a Coin

In 1903, Orville and Wilbur were arguing over who would get to fly first. They decided to flip a coin to see who would win the honor. Wilbur won the toss, but his flight was unsuccessful, and he damaged the plane. After some repairs, it was Orville's turn. He was in the air for just 12 seconds before he had to touch back down.

original 1903
Wright Flyer

The Wrights kept making small improvements. By 1903, they had invented the first successful airplane. But their flights were straight and short. If pilots wanted to turn the planes, they had to move their hips left or right to twist the wings a certain way. The Wrights knew this would not work. Their next step was to discover an easier way to turn the plane.

The Wrights made two more planes. By 1905, they had a plane that could fly for several minutes at a time and could turn without the use of anyone's hips. On October 5, Wilbur stayed in the air for 39 minutes as he circled a field over and over again. The dawn of flight had officially begun.

Europe Flies High

Even after the Wright brothers' 1903 trip to the skies, many people still did not think flight was possible. So Wilbur went to Europe in 1908 to show them what he and his brother had made. People in Europe were impressed! Orville joined Wilbur the next year, and they were treated like celebrities.

Farnsworth's TV

The first versions of the television came out in the early 1920s. But it took a man named Philo Farnsworth to make modern TV happen. He originally had an idea in high school for a way to improve TV by using vacuum tubes. He tried to show his teachers, but they couldn't understand his new concept. But that didn't stop Farnsworth.

After high school, Farnsworth went to college. But he had to drop out after his father died. Farnsworth had to get a job to help pay the bills, but that did not stop him from experimenting. In 1927, he finished his all-electronic TV prototype. It was the same device he had thought of in high school!

The Magic of Mold

In 1928, Sir Alexander Fleming (shown above) was cleaning his messy lab. He had been trying to come up with a drug that would treat **infections**. He noticed that the bacteria he'd been growing was gone. Instead, mold had begun to grow there. Fleming had discovered penicillin! But no one took much notice of his findings. It would take 10 years for it to become a common treatment for bacteria.

Penicillin

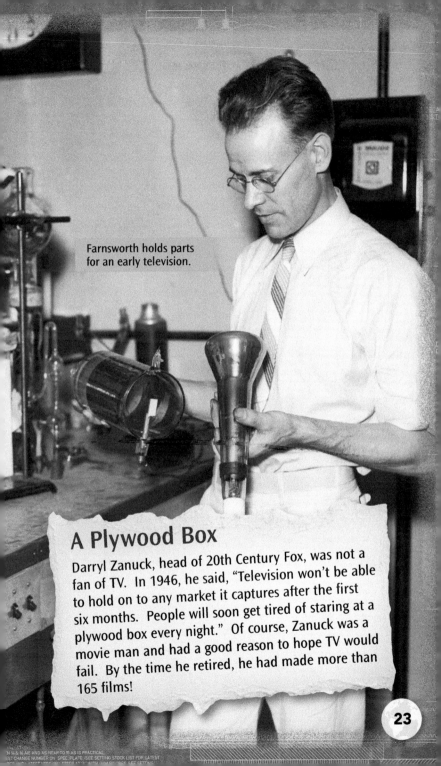

Farnsworth holds parts for an early television.

A Plywood Box

Darryl Zanuck, head of 20th Century Fox, was not a fan of TV. In 1946, he said, "Television won't be able to hold on to any market it captures after the first six months. People will soon get tired of staring at a plywood box every night." Of course, Zanuck was a movie man and had a good reason to hope TV would fail. By the time he retired, he had made more than 165 films!

'N 14 & 16 A/E AND AS NEAR TO 15 AS IS PRACTICAL.
EST CHANGE NUMBER ON SPEC. PLATE. (SEE SETTING STOCK LIST FOR LATEST

Carlson's Copy Machine

Chester Carlson's job was to make copies of papers. His only two options were to pay to make expensive copies or to have the documents retyped. Carlson knew there had to be a better way. So in 1934, he began to try new ways of making copies.

It only took a few years before Carlson discovered the science behind making exact copies. He just needed a machine to carry out the process. For six years, he searched for a company to build his machine. During that time, over 20 companies turned him down. Finally, a company agreed. That company would later be known as Xerox®.

Finding the Bug

One day in 1944, while working in the lab, Grace Hopper (shown below) saw that a machine was not working properly. The machine was the Mark I—an early computer that was more than 50 feet (15 meters) long. Hopper had helped build Mark I, so it did not take her long to find the problem. A moth had flown in to the machine and was causing the failure. Hopper coined the term *bug* (a term still used today) to refer to anything that causes a computer to malfunction.

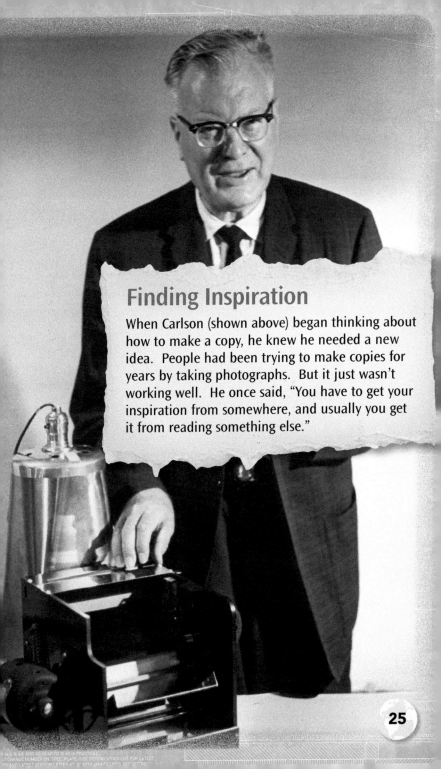

Finding Inspiration

When Carlson (shown above) began thinking about how to make a copy, he knew he needed a new idea. People had been trying to make copies for years by taking photographs. But it just wasn't working well. He once said, "You have to get your inspiration from somewhere, and usually you get it from reading something else."

Spencer's Melting Magnetrons

One day in 1945, Percy Spencer was walking in his lab. As he passed a machine called a *magnetron*, something strange happened. The candy bar in his pocket started to melt.

Spencer wanted to know what effect the magnetron might have on other foods. So, he began experimenting with the machine. Popcorn kernels flew all over his lab. An egg exploded in his face. The next year, his company built a machine called the *Radarange*. But it was 6 feet (2 meters) tall and weighed almost 700 pounds (320 kilograms)! It took another 20 years before microwaves were available for home use.

Instant Pictures

In 1943, Edwin Land took a photo of his three-year old daughter. She wanted to see the picture, which gave Land a great idea. It took Land four years to **perfect** his invention. In 1947, Land debuted the Polaroid Land Camera.

POLAROID LAND CAMERA

Velvet and Hooks

When Georges de Mestral (day mez-TRAHL) and his dog went for a walk in the woods in 1941, they came home covered in sticky burrs. De Mestral looked at the burrs under a microscope and thought he could make similar hooks and loops. First made from cotton and then from nylon, VELCRO® caught on in a big way. It is used on everything from children's shoes to space shuttles.

Late 1900s and Beyond: Speed

If the inventions of the early 1900s were about comfort and convenience, inventions in the second half of the century were focused on doing things faster and better.

The Bar Code

In 1949, Joe Woodland was thinking while sitting on a beach. He was trying to come up with a faster way to check out at the grocery store. Until then, cashiers had to find each item's price and type it into the register one at a time. As Woodland thought, he pulled his fingers through the sand. As he drew four lines, a thought struck him—Woodland could use thick and thin lines as codes. He knew he was on to something big. Now, he just needed a machine to read the code.

Summer Sports

In 1980, brothers Scott and Brennan Olson were looking for a way to keep playing hockey in the summer. They saw a pair of in-line skates at a sporting goods store and thought it was just what they needed. The brothers purchased the patent and improved the design. They released their new product, called Rollerblades®, and skated to success.

Formula for Success

Formula 409® is one of the best-selling cleaning products in the United States, but the invention did not come easy. Two young scientists were determined to make the best cleaner in the world. It took hundreds of tries to get it right. On the 409th attempt, they finally agreed that their product was perfect.

Woodland turned to his friend Bernard Silver for help, and the two worked together to build a code reader. It worked, but it was the size of a desk. In order to be useful, it had to be much smaller. And the light they were using to read the codes was not strong enough. They needed technology to catch up with their idea. Finally, in 1960, it did.

A scientist named Theodore Maiman (MAY-muhn) made a light that was said to be "brighter than the sun." Maiman called it a LASER, which stood for *Light Amplification by Stimulated Emission of Radiation*. Woodland and Silver knew this was the break they needed. Now, they just had to put it all together.

A Poisonous Problem

In 1964, a ship in Kuwait tipped over with more than five thousand sheep aboard. People were worried that the animals would poison their water supply. Karl Kroyer decided to try to raise the ship by filling it with millions of small foam balls, to help it float. The idea worked! The problem caused by the failure of the ship inspired Kroyer to come up with a creative solution.

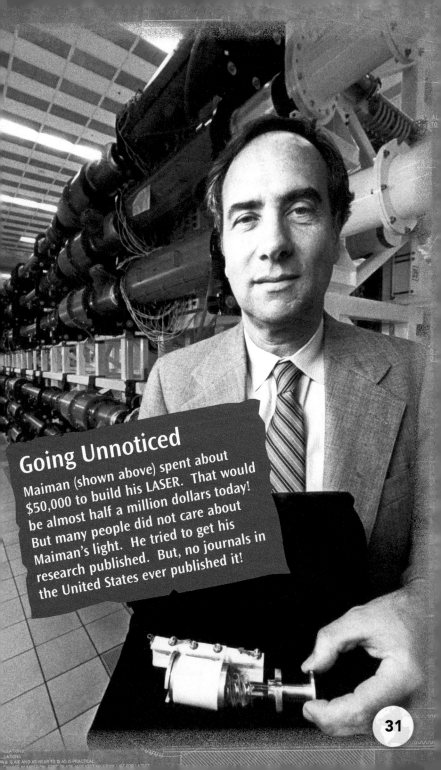

Going Unnoticed

Maiman (shown above) spent about $50,000 to build his LASER. That would be almost half a million dollars today! But many people did not care about Maiman's light. He tried to get his research published. But, no journals in the United States ever published it!

Checkout Ideas

Grocery store owners spent years trying to find a way to improve their checkout systems. At some stores, customers used punch cards to mark which items they wanted to buy. Then, the cashier would go get the items for them. In other stores, shoppers put everything into one basket and pushed it under a scanner. But scanners were not able to identify each item. Neither of these ideas lasted.

In 1972, a research team used Maiman's LASER to read Woodland and Silver's bar codes at a Kroger® grocery store in Cincinnati, Ohio. The system was a big hit! Customers could check out much faster. And Kroger could sell more products.

But bar codes were different depending on which store you were in. Grocery store owners thought it would be too hard to keep track of all of the different codes at all of their stores.

In 1973, IBM developed **universal** bar codes. Soon after, they built lasers that would read the codes. For the first time, IBM's Universal Product Codes (UPC) made it so products could be scanned anywhere. Stores raced to adopt the bar code technology. Shopping would never be the same.

Bull's-Eye!

When Woodland was drawing in the sand that fateful day, he originally drew his bar code as a circle. The bull's-eye design was almost impossible to print correctly. But circles were used on bar codes until IBM got involved. They changed the circle into a rectangle, which is still the shape used today.

937900 203229

Left to right: Atari founders Ted Dabney and Nolan Bushnell with Fred Marincheck (finances) and Al Alcorn (game design).

Stolen Ideas?

In 1972, the world's first video game system was released. The Magnavox Odyssey (shown below) came with a ping-pong game. This game inspired Bushnell and Dabney to create their game, *Pong*. Two years after *Pong*'s release, the makers of the Magnavox Odyssey sued Atari for stealing their idea. Magnavox won the court case in 1977, but by then, *Pong* was too big to matter.

Popularity of Pong

While Maiman was building his LASER, two men were working on a different invention that would change the world. Computer games had been around since 1961. But they were not available to the public until 1971. That's when Nolan Bushnell and Ted Dabney made their first arcade game. They sold the game, *Computer Space*, to a machine maker. But people found it hard to operate.

Bushnell and Dabney refused to give up. In 1972, they started their own business, called Atari®. That same year, they built a second arcade game. They installed the machine in a local restaurant. It was a huge hit, and everyone wanted to play. In the first year, Atari sold eight thousand *Pong* machines.

Slap Bracelets

In 1983, Stuart Anders was playing with steel ribbons when he got an idea. He covered the ribbons in fabric and sold them as bracelets, which he called "Slap Wraps." He had many failures. He had to change his design so that people wouldn't cut themselves on sharp metal edges. Other companies tried to steal his idea. Anders didn't give up. He kept selling his bracelets and became a success. In 1990, Slap Wraps made about $15,000,000.

Post-It Notes

Dr. Spencer Silver wanted to create strong glue, but his formula was off. His glue wasn't strong; it was just sticky. Silver thought it could be useful, but many people told him to stop wasting his time with it.

Silver showed his glue to Art Fry, one of his coworkers at 3M. Fry began experimenting and discovered it could hold two pieces of paper together without tearing the pages. Fry knew he was onto something and convinced his company to let him test out his idea.

In 1978, 3M tested a product called "Press'n Peel." Some people really liked the product, but overall sales were discouraging. Then 3M changed the name of the note pads to "Post-it® Notes." They sold 50 million packs in the first year.

Little Failures Make Big Leaps

James Dyson invented the first bagless vacuum. But it was not an easy road for him. Dyson failed 5,127 times before getting it right. He said the design process includes "little failures [that] let engineers make big leaps."

Art Fry

Just Try

"If I had thought about it, I wouldn't have done the experiment. The literature was full of examples that said you can't do this."

—Spencer Silver, on the work that led to Post-it Notes

The World Wide Web

You may never have heard of Tim Berners-Lee. But, people can use his invention to learn more about him. Just open up a web browser and type his name in the search window. Pages will show up with pictures of Berners-Lee and articles about his life. These pages and countless others can by found the same way by people all over the world.

1989

The World Wide Web is invented by Tim Berners-Lee. The first website goes online.

1996

Nokia introduces the Nok[i] 9000 Communicator, whic[h] is the first phone that cou[ld] connect to the Internet.

1990   1995   200[0]

1990

my search

Archie—the Internet's first search engine—goes online, eight years before Google.

2004

Mark Zuckerberg puts Facebook online.

This system of linked text, images, and videos is called the **World Wide Web**. It makes up a large part of what most people use the Internet for today. Berners-Lee's invention has given many people a tool to use the Internet in different ways. Here is a time line of some of the major events that have shaped our culture thanks to the World Wide Web.

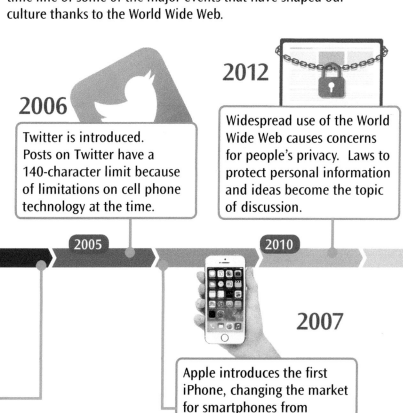

2006

Twitter is introduced. Posts on Twitter have a 140-character limit because of limitations on cell phone technology at the time.

2012

Widespread use of the World Wide Web causes concerns for people's privacy. Laws to protect personal information and ideas become the topic of discussion.

2005

2010

2007

Apple introduces the first iPhone, changing the market for smartphones from business use to mainstream markets.

A Future Like No Other

Every day, we depend on inventions to do just about everything. Where would we be without clocks, toilets, refrigerators, cars, and computers? The list of inventions that we would find it hard to live without is very long.

But not all inventors got it right on their first tries. Far from it! Invention is a process of trial and error, followed by more trial and more error. There is no doubt that future inventors will fail, too. But they must keep trying after every failure. People who believe in their ideas should never give up!

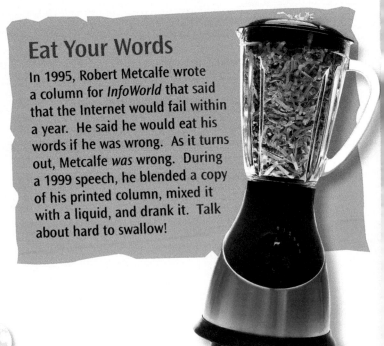

Eat Your Words

In 1995, Robert Metcalfe wrote a column for *InfoWorld* that said that the Internet would fail within a year. He said he would eat his words if he was wrong. As it turns out, Metcalfe *was* wrong. During a 1999 speech, he blended a copy of his printed column, mixed it with a liquid, and drank it. Talk about hard to swallow!

Becoming an Inventor: 101

If you have an idea that you think can change the world, the first step is to test it out. It is important to keep a record of your successes and failures along the way. Build a prototype, and keep improving your design. Then, file a patent, and go sell your invention!

Glossary

alternative—something that can be chosen over another option

astronomer—a person who studies stars, planets, and other objects in outer space

asylum—a hospital where people who are mentally ill are cared for

compute—to solve something by using math processes

crank—a person with strange ideas

criticism—the act of noting the problems or faults of a person or thing

dejected—feeling very sad

fascinated—caused someone to be very interested in another person or thing

filament—a thin wire in a light bulb that allows electricity to pass through

glider—an aircraft similar to an airplane but without an engine

humid—having a lot of moisture in the atmosphere

infections—diseases caused by germs

invest—to use money to make more money

Morse code—a system of sending messages that uses sounds, light, or marks to represent letters and numbers

patents—documents that give a person or company the right to be the only one that makes or sells a certain product

perfect—to make something perfect or to make it better

prototype—an original or first model of something

radiation—a type of dangerous and powerful energy that comes from radioactive substances and nuclear reactions

ridicule—the act of making fun of something or someone in a harsh or cruel way

rivals—people who compete against one another

shortcomings— failure to meet certain standards, usually describing a person's character or a plan

strokes—serious illnesses caused when a blood vessel in the brain becomes blocked or broken

telegraph—an old-fashioned system of sending messages over long distances by using wires and electrical signals

universal—the same in all times or places

World Wide Web—part of the Internet containing documents often connected by hyperlinks

Index

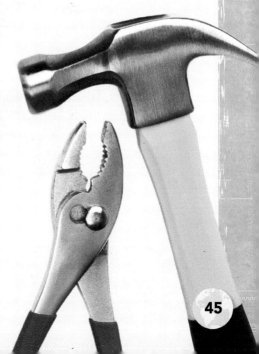

Check It Out!

Books

Bender, Lionel. 2013. *Invention*. New York: DK Children.

Popular Mechanics. 2014. *Popular Mechanics Gadget Planet: 150 Gizmos & Inventions That Changed the World*. New York: Hearst.

Turner, Tracey, Andrea Mills, and Clive Gifford. 2014. *100 Inventions That Made History: Brilliant Breakthroughs That Shaped Our World*. New York: DK Children.

Websites

Inventive Kids. www.inventivekids.com/

Zoom Inventors and Inventions. Enchanted Learning. www.enchantedlearning.com/inventors/

Try It!

Imagine you are an inventor. A research company has hired you to solve a problem in your community.

⚙ Make a list of things that could be made better or ways to improve the lives of people in your community.

⚙ Next, choose one issue. Research what has been done to fix the problem. Is there already an existing idea or invention you can modify? Or, will you have to start from scratch?

⚙ Draw your prototype. Show your drawing to your classmates and ask if they see any ways to improve upon your design.

⚙ Write a brief description of the problem, how your invention will solve the problem, and attach your final prototype drawing. Be sure to name your invention.

About the Author

Jody Jensen Shaffer loves a great idea, even if it doesn't succeed on the first attempt. She's the author of more than 30 books for children. Shaffer also writes poetry and fiction for children's magazines in the United States and internationally. She works from her home in Missouri.